T0398157

THE AMAZING HUMAN BODY

THE HUMAN
MUSCULAR SYSTEM

by Samantha S. Bell

BrightP◆int Press

San Diego, CA

© 2025 BrightPoint Press

an imprint of ReferencePoint Press, Inc.

Printed in the United States

For more information, contact:

BrightPoint Press

PO Box 27779

San Diego, CA 92198

www.BrightPointPress.com

LIBRARY OF CONGRESS CATALOGING-IN-PUBLICATION DATA

Name: Bell, Samantha S., author.

Title: The human muscular system / by Samantha S. Bell.

Description: San Diego, CA: BrightPoint Press, 2025 | Series: The amazing human body | Audience: Grade 7 to 9 | Includes bibliographical references and index.

Identifiers: ISBN: 9781678209605 (hardcover) | ISBN: 9781678209612 (eBook)

The complete Library of Congress record is available at www.loc.gov.

CONTENTS

AT A GLANCE

- The muscular system is made up of muscles. These soft tissues work together to move the body.

- Muscles are attached to bones and organs. Muscles move the body by contracting and relaxing.

- The three types of muscles are skeletal muscles, smooth muscles, and cardiac muscles.

- Skeletal muscles are voluntary. Smooth and cardiac muscles are involuntary.

- Muscle contraction is controlled by the nervous system, which includes the brain, spinal cord, and nerves.

- Muscle atrophy is the loss of muscle tissue. It causes muscles to look smaller and become weaker.

- Exercise can increase muscle mass, strength, and endurance.

- Proper nutrition is important for keeping muscles healthy and strong.

- Protein helps build and repair muscle tissues.

BREAKING RECORDS

It is the 2009 World Athletics Championships in Berlin, Germany. The sprinters line up at the starting line. The crowd cheers as the sprinters are introduced. Among them are Usain Bolt, Tyson Gay, and Asafa Powell. They are about to race the 100-meter dash.

Bolt is a sprinter from Jamaica. He already holds the world record. In 2008, he ran the 100-meter dash in the

Seven years after competing in Berlin, Bolt earned three gold medals at the 2016 Olympic Games in Rio de Janeiro, Brazil.

Olympic Games. He finished in only 9.69 seconds. Beside Bolt is Gay. He is the American record holder for the 100-meter dash. Powell is a former world-record holder. In 2009, these athletes were the three fastest men in the world.

The race starts. Bolt pulls out in front of the others. He holds his head high.

Sprinters typically reach their top speed at around 180 to 210 feet (55 to 65 m). After that, they begin to slow down as their muscles tire.

He pumps his arms rapidly. His legs push him forward with explosive power. Bolt finishes the race in first place. His time is 9.58 seconds. He has set a new world record.

A SPRINTER'S MUSCLES

Bolt ran at an average speed of about 23.4 miles per hour (37.6 kmh). He was able to run that fast thanks to his muscles. Muscles make up the muscular system. The muscular system allows the body to move. Each muscle moves a particular part of the body. Scientists have named more than 600 muscles in the human muscular system.

Muscles are made of strong fibers. The fibers tighten to move the body. But the fibers are not all the same. There are two main types of muscle fibers. Some fibers are slow-twitch fibers. They use energy slowly. The body uses these fibers for movements made over a long period of time. Others are fast-twitch fibers. These fibers create large amounts of force in a short amount of time. They help the body make sudden, powerful movements. Sprinters like Bolt have a lot of fast-twitch muscle fibers.

Muscles perform many functions throughout the body. Humans need their muscles in order to move, breathe, and digest food. A strong muscular system helps people live active, healthy lives.

Fast-twitch muscles create short, powerful bursts of force, which is helpful when lifting weights.

CHAPTER ONE

WHAT IS THE MUSCULAR SYSTEM?

Muscles are a type of soft **tissue**. They are attached to the body's bones and organs. Muscles contract to produce movement. When a muscle contracts, it tightens. It becomes shorter. This allows muscles to pull a body part in a direction. Even when people sit very still, some of their muscles are contracting. This keeps people from falling over.

When people flex their muscles, the muscles don't actually get larger. Instead, contraction makes the muscles bulge as they shorten.

Muscles come in many different shapes and sizes. One of the smallest muscles is located inside the ear. It's called the stapedius. It is about 0.35 to 0.43 inches (9 to 11 mm) long. It supports the smallest bone in the body, the stapes. The stapedius

Goose bumps occur due to very small involuntary muscles in the skin.

helps dampen sounds that enter the inner ear. This protects the ear from damage.

The largest muscle in the human body is the gluteus maximus. This is the muscle people sit on. It runs from the hip bone to the thigh bone. D. Ceri Davies is a professor of anatomy. Anatomy is the study of the body structure of living things. Davies explains that we use this muscle as we get up from a chair or walk uphill. He says, "It needs to be powerful to move the weight of the entire upper body."[1]

Muscles may be voluntary or involuntary. Voluntary muscles are muscles that people can control. People decide when to move these muscles. They are used for actions such as walking and chewing.

Involuntary muscles do their jobs on their own. People do not have to think about moving them. These muscles are constantly active. Involuntary muscles include the muscles that make the heart beat. They also include the muscles that move food through the digestive system.

Some body functions use both voluntary and involuntary muscles. For example,

Muscles of the Eye

Six muscles move the eye. One muscle moves the eye up. Another moves it down. One turns it toward the nose. Another turns it outward. The last two muscles rotate the eye. These muscles are constantly adjusting the eye's position. For example, they make nearly 10,000 movements when someone reads for an hour.

voluntary muscles control the movement of the eye. But involuntary muscles control the size of the pupil. This is the dark opening in the middle of the eye. It affects how much light enters the eye.

TYPES OF MUSCLES

There are three types of muscles. The first is skeletal muscle. Skeletal muscles look like bundles of fibers. Each skeletal muscle contains hundreds or thousands of fibers. The fibers are grouped together. Each group is surrounded by tissue called a sheath. Together, the bundles of fibers form the whole muscle.

Skeletal muscles are all voluntary muscles. They are attached to bones by tendons. Tendons are tough cords of tissue.

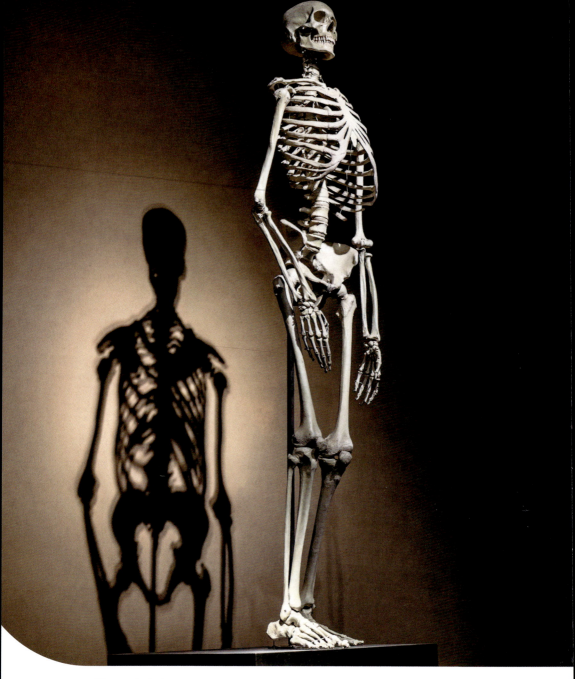

The adult human skeleton has about 206 bones. Some people have more or less due to small natural variations.

When skeletal muscles contract, they move bones. This allows **limbs** and other body parts to move. Most of the body's muscles are skeletal muscles.

The second type of muscle is smooth muscle. Smooth muscles line blood vessels and organs. They are involuntary. Smooth muscles perform many important functions. Some smooth muscles are in the stomach and the intestines. These muscles help move food through the digestive system. They also help collect nutrients from food. Smooth muscles are found in the **urinary system** as well. They help move waste and extra water out of the body. Smooth muscles in arteries and veins help control blood flow.

The third type of muscle is cardiac muscle. Cardiac muscles are located only in the heart. Like smooth muscles, they are involuntary. They are made up of special cells. These cells contract to squeeze the heart. This creates the pressure needed to pump blood through the body.

The heart has four chambers. The lower chambers are called the left and right ventricles. The upper chambers are called the left and right atria. The muscles in the chambers are not all the same. Ellen Roche is a biomedical engineer. She explains that the muscles of the left ventricle must pump blood through the whole body. The muscles of the right ventricle only pump blood to the lungs. This means that the two ventricles have different muscles. She says, "The right

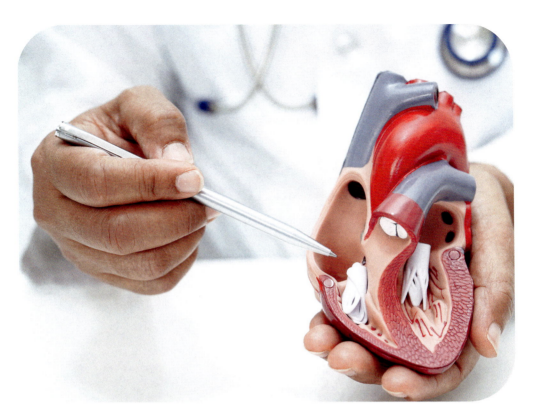

Blood picks up oxygen in the lungs. Then blood travels to the heart, which pumps it to the rest of the body.

ventricle . . . doesn't have to pump as hard. It's a thinner muscle, with more complex [structure] and motion."[2]

THE MANY ROLES OF MUSCLES

Different types of muscles have different jobs in the body. Skeletal muscles work with the bones to help the body move. They also

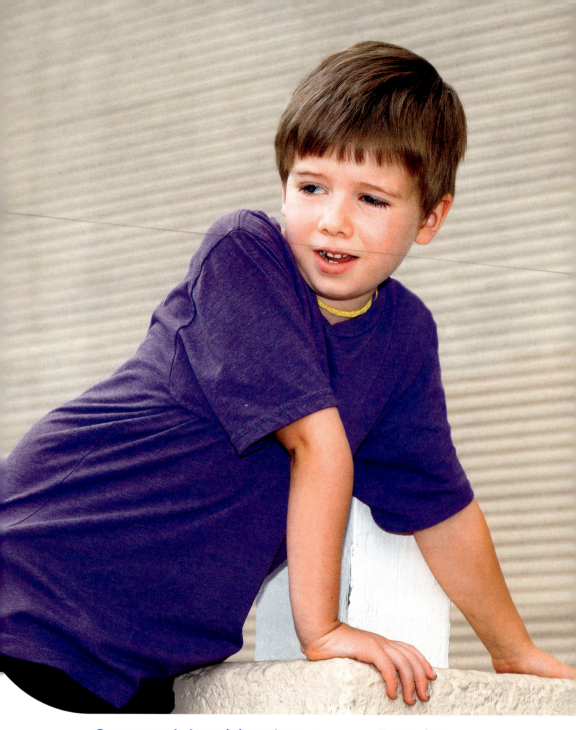

Some people have joints that are unusually flexible. This condition is called joint hypermobility, or double-jointedness.

help control movement around the **joints**. Some muscles have tendons that go over joints, such as the knees and shoulders.

Skeletal muscles produce heat when they contract. This is because muscles make heat when they use the body's energy. This helps the body maintain its normal temperature of 97.3 to 98.2°F (36.3 to 37.8°C). Nearly 85 percent of heat produced in the body is from muscles. Muscles shiver to make extra heat when the body is cold. They do this by quickly contracting and relaxing.

Some muscles are deep in the **abdomen**, hips, and back. These are called core muscles. They help people maintain their posture. These muscles are

Hiccups happen when the diaphragm involuntarily contracts. Eating a large meal or drinking fizzy beverages can cause hiccups.

constantly adjusting to keep someone in a sitting or standing position.

Muscles play an important role in breathing. The diaphragm is a large, strong muscle. It is located between the lungs and the abdomen. It is the main muscle at work when people breathe. It moves downward to draw in air and expand the lungs. Then it moves upward to push out air. When people exercise, they may breathe heavier. In this case, other muscles may help the diaphragm. These can include the back, neck, and abdominal muscles.

CHAPTER TWO

HOW DOES THE MUSCULAR SYSTEM WORK?

Muscles move the body by contracting and relaxing. These movements are controlled by the nervous system. The nervous system is made up of all the nerve cells in the body. It includes the brain and spinal cord. The nervous system takes in information through the senses. It processes the information. Then it produces reactions, such as making muscles move.

Nerve signals travel to muscles at speeds of up to 270 miles per hour (440 kmh).

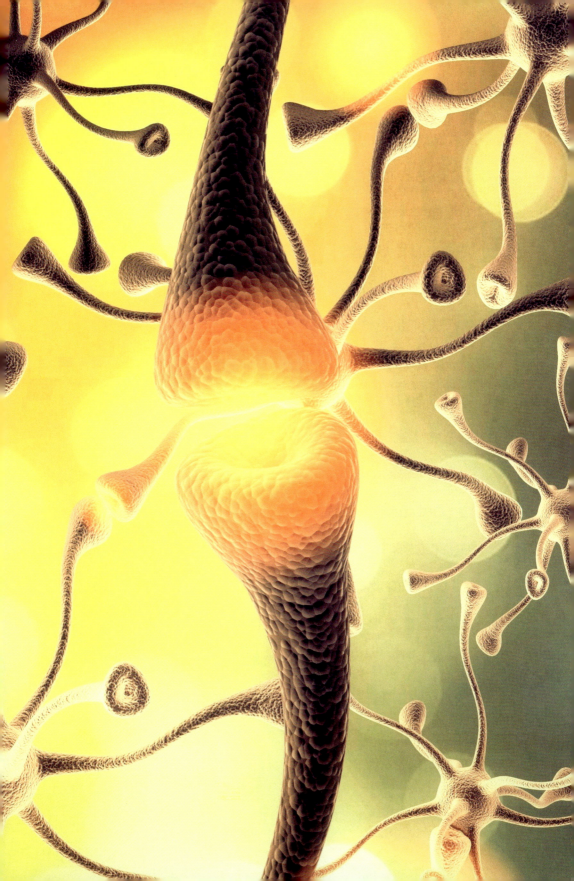

Nerves called motor neurons connect the brain to the muscles. Motor neurons run down the spine. Then they branch out to each muscle. The brain sends signals to muscles using motor neurons.

Voluntary muscles and involuntary muscles are controlled by different parts of the brain. When someone decides to move, the brain sends voluntary muscles a signal. The nerve fibers tell the muscles to contract or relax. To control involuntary muscles, the brain sends signals automatically. Involuntary muscles may also contract in response to their environment. For example, smooth muscles in the digestion system contract when food is in the body.

CONTRACTION

Skeletal muscles pull on tendons. The tendons move bones. But skeletal muscles pull in only one direction. They cannot push the bone back. For this reason, skeletal muscles always come in pairs. One muscle

Organs of the digestive system, such as the stomach and intestines, are lined with muscles. These muscles contract to push food through the system.

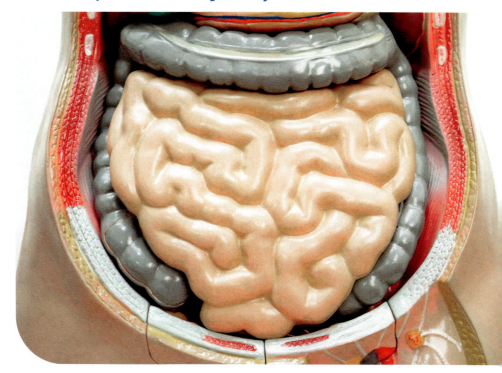

contracts to bend a limb at a joint. Then the muscle relaxes. The other muscle contracts. The limb straightens out once again.

For example, bending an arm at the elbow takes two muscles. These muscles are called the biceps and the triceps. First, the biceps contracts. It pulls the forearm toward the shoulder. But when the biceps relaxes, it cannot push the arm

Strength Competitions

Each year, people from around the world enter strength competitions. These competitions involve many different challenges. Contestants may have to flip huge metal poles or carry heavy stones. They may race with refrigerators strapped to their backs. They may even pull a truck or a boat using a cable. The athletes train for these challenges by strengthening their muscles.

out again. Instead, the triceps contracts. It pulls the elbow the other way. The arm straightens out.

A muscle's strength depends mainly on how many fibers it contains. If a person tries to move a heavy object, the body will contract enough muscle fibers to do the job. It will use more fibers if the object is heavy. But the weight may be greater than the force made by all the fibers. In this case, the person will not be able to move the object.

Muscle contraction also causes the heart to beat. The heart must move blood throughout the whole body. To do this, cardiac muscles contract with powerful force. This force pushes blood out of the heart. Other muscles help keep the

Lifting a heavy object improperly can strain the back. That's why experts recommend people squat and use their legs to lift.

blood moving. These include smooth muscle cells in the walls of blood vessels.

FUELING THE MUSCLES

Muscles need energy to contract. Without enough energy, the muscles do not work as well as they should. Carbohydrates are the main fuel source of muscles. Carbohydrates are a nutrient found in food. Foods high in carbohydrates include bread and crackers. They also include beans, fruit, and nuts. The body breaks carbohydrates down into a chemical called glucose. Glucose provides energy to the muscles. It is stored in the muscles or the **liver**. The body uses it later for energy.

The body breaks down glucose when it needs energy. This produces a chemical called adenosine triphosphate (ATP). ATP is like a tiny packet of energy. Wes Dudgeon is an exercise science professor. He says, "Any time a muscle moves, ATP is used. That's the only fuel that our muscles can use to contract."[3]

Dietitians are experts who help people make healthy eating choices. Dietitians recommend that people make carbohydrates 45 to 65 percent of their diet.

Muscle cells contain two special **proteins**. They are called myosin and actin. These proteins help muscles contract. Muscles receive signals from the nervous system. Then, a mineral called calcium rushes into the muscle. The calcium allows actin and myosin to work. ATP also helps these proteins interact with each other. This process results in muscle contraction.

CHAPTER THREE

WHAT CAN GO WRONG WITH THE MUSCULAR SYSTEM?

One problem that affects the muscular system is muscle spasms. These occur when voluntary muscles contract on their own. Spasms can range from mild to severe. In mild cases, the muscle may seem to twitch. In severe cases, it may feel like it has become a tight ball. Muscle spasms can be very painful.

A muscle spasm may last for a few seconds. If it lasts longer, it is called a

One way to treat a muscle spasm or cramp is to gently massage the muscle.

It is important to drink enough water when exercising in hot weather. Not getting enough water can lead to heat exhaustion, which can be life-threatening if untreated.

muscle cramp. Cramps can last up to 15 minutes or longer. Cramps that last a long time can make muscles sore even after the cramps are gone.

Spasms and cramps can involve just part of a muscle. They can also affect a whole muscle. Some cramps even involve several muscles. They can happen anywhere on the body. Some common areas where spasms and cramps happen include the back and arms. They also happen in the legs, chest, and abdomen.

Muscle spasms and cramps can happen at any time. They can occur while a person is exercising, sitting, or even sleeping. Some groups of people are more likely to get them. These include athletes who exercise for long periods of time. People older than

65 years old might get cramps if they become too hot or **dehydrated**. So might babies and young children. People who are pregnant or overweight have an increased risk of muscle spasms too. Some people get them because of diseases or other health conditions.

Experts are not sure why some people get muscle spasms more than others. Some causes of spasms may include sitting for long periods of time or not stretching enough. People who exercise in extreme heat may get spasms. Stress can also cause spasms.

MUSCLE STRAINS

A muscle strain is an injury to a muscle or tendon. It is sometimes called a

pulled muscle. Sometimes the strained muscle or tendon is overstretched. Other times, the tissue is torn.

Strained muscles can be painful. They can cause redness, bruises, or swelling. A strain can make the muscle weak. It can also limit the muscle's range of motion.

A strain can be caused by a single action. For example, a person might try to lift a very heavy object. This effort could put a lot of force on the muscles in the person's back. This could result in a strain.

People who play paddle sports such as tennis can strain their elbows when swinging hard. That's why this kind of strain is sometimes called *tennis elbow*.

A muscle can also be strained over time. This can happen when a person repeats the same motion many times. These strains are called chronic muscle strains. They often affect athletes. Soccer and football players may strain their legs and ankles. Gymnasts and golfers can strain the muscles in their hands. Playing tennis can cause elbow strains.

Muscles that have more fast-twitch fibers strain more easily. Fast-twitch fibers contract quickly to create more power. Joel Cramer is a professor at the University of Nebraska. He explains, "It's relatively uncommon for [slow-twitch muscles] to strain. They're used to being active all the time."[4]

MUSCLE ATROPHY

Sometimes people lose muscle tissue over time. This is called muscle atrophy. The muscles become smaller than normal. They also become weaker. People with muscle atrophy may have a hard time keeping their balance. They may fall often or have trouble walking. Some may not be able to raise their arms or reach for high objects. They may not be able to hold a pen or type on a computer.

Muscle atrophy can occur when muscles are not used enough. Muscles require a lot of energy. To save energy, the body breaks down muscles it does not use. This causes the muscles to decrease in size and strength. Atrophy can happen when people do not get enough exercise. It can

Physical therapy is a medical treatment that can help people suffering from muscular disorders move with more freedom and less pain.

also happen to people with health problems that limit their movement. For example, a **stroke** can affect people's ability to use their muscles.

Some muscle loss is a natural part of getting older. People lose as much as 3 to 5 percent of their muscle mass each decade after age 30. Jodi Klein is a physical therapist. Klein says, "People older than age 65 are especially vulnerable to muscle atrophy."[5]

Serious types of muscle atrophy are caused by injuries or diseases. These conditions affect the nerves connected to muscles. Damaged nerves may not be able to trigger muscle contractions. This can result in atrophy. For example, multiple

Living with MS

Selma Blair is an actress. She was diagnosed with MS in 2018. For a while, she dropped things she was holding. Sometimes she fell down. She also had trouble thinking clearly. Then she found a treatment that helped. In 2021, she said that her disease had gone into remission. This eased some of her symptoms. However, she was still in pain most of the time. She also had spasms.

sclerosis (MS) is a disease that damages the nerve fibers in the brain and spinal cord. As a result, people with MS may have muscle weakness. Other symptoms can include blurred vision and spasms. The symptoms can come and go. They may even change over time.

CHAPTER FOUR

WHAT CAN HUMANS DO TO KEEP THE MUSCULAR SYSTEM HEALTHY?

There are ways that people can keep their muscles healthy and strong. One such way is by staying active. This is true for people of any age. People who sit most of the day should try to find time for exercise. Almost any activity that moves the body will improve muscle health.

Staying active can also help people regain muscle they have lost. Even older adults can regain muscle. Jodi Klein says,

The US Department of Health and Human Services recommends that most children and teenagers get at least 60 minutes of exercise per day.

"With the right strategy, older adults can protect themselves from muscle atrophy and rebound easier if it occurs."[6]

A simple way to work the muscles is by stretching. Stretching improves flexibility. This gives muscles a greater range of motion. This also reduces the risk

Many people use yoga as a stretching exercise.

of injury. Muscles may become short and tight when people do not stretch enough. The muscles cannot extend as far as they might be able to if regularly stretched. For example, sitting all day can cause the muscles in the back of the thigh to tighten. This can make it harder to stand up or walk.

People should find time to stretch during the day. They may choose to stretch after waking up. They can also stretch before bed. Some people stretch during breaks at work. It is also good to stretch after exercising. Lynn Millar is a physical therapist and professor. She says, "Everyone is more flexible after exercise, because you've increased the circulation to those muscles and joints and you've been moving them."[7]

BUILDING MUSCLE

Another way people can keep their muscles healthy is by strengthening them. Certain exercises increase muscle size and strength. The goal of these exercises is to increase the amount of muscle mass in the body. Raising muscle mass improves movement, balance, and endurance. It also allows people to lift heavier objects.

People can choose to focus on strengthening specific muscle groups. They may use weights in a gym. They can also use their own body weight. For example, push-ups are an exercise people can do almost anywhere. Push-ups involve working against one's own body weight. This exercise strengthens the muscles in the arms and shoulders.

Exercise can cause tiny tears to form in muscle fibers. These are called microtears. Microtears cause people to feel sore. The body sends extra nutrients and blood to that area. This creates more muscle fibers. The muscle mass increases. Michael Karns is a doctor. He says, "You have to break muscle down to build it back up stronger."[8]

The RICE Method

The RICE method is one way people treat strained muscles. *RICE* stands for rest, ice, compression, and elevation. First, the person should rest the muscle. Then they should apply ice for a short time. Compression means using an elastic bandage to wrap the muscle. Finally, they should keep the muscle lifted above heart level. These actions reduce pain and swelling.

BODY-WEIGHT EXERCISES

PUSH-UPS
Upper body, core

PLANKS
Upper body, core, lower body

CRUNCHES
Core

SQUATS
Lower body

HIGH KNEES
Core, lower body

LUNGES
Lower body

Body-weight exercises can work muscles throughout the human body.

People must exercise regularly to build muscle. But muscles also need time to recover after a workout. The microtears need a day or two to heal. Muscles do not grow as strong without recovery. The risk of injury also rises.

GOOD NUTRITION

Proteins are substances found in all living things. Proteins do most of the work in cells. They help build and repair muscles and tissues. They keep all parts of the body functioning properly. This includes the muscles.

Proteins are made up of smaller substances called amino acids. Cells use amino acids to build new proteins. The body can make some amino acids itself. Other amino acids come from the protein in food. People must eat enough food to keep their muscles healthy. Not eating enough protein causes muscle atrophy.

Protein comes from both animal and plant sources. These include meats such as chicken and beef. Eggs are another

Dietitians recommend that people make protein 10 to 35 percent of their diet.

good source of protein. Beans and other legumes are a good plant source. Foods that contain protein help people feel full for a longer time.

Eating well and exercising help keep the muscular system healthy. People should talk to a doctor if they notice unusual or extreme symptoms in their muscles. These symptoms include pain that does not go away and a limited range of motion. Keeping the muscular system in good shape is very important. Healthy muscles allow people to live energetically.

GLOSSARY

abdomen

the part of the body between the chest and the hips

dehydrated

having less water in the body than it needs

joints

places in the body where at least two bones meet

limbs

arms and legs

liver

an organ that processes nutrients and removes waste from the blood

proteins

complex substances that living things use to perform chemical functions

stroke

a medical condition in which the flow of blood to part of the brain is interrupted

tissue

a group of similar cells that together perform a specific function

urinary system

a body system that removes waste and extra fluid

SOURCE NOTES

CHAPTER ONE: WHAT IS THE MUSCULAR SYSTEM?

1. Quoted in Anna Gora, "What's the Largest Muscle in the Body, and the Smallest?," *LiveScience*, October 8, 2023. www.livescience.com.

2. Quoted in Jennifer Chu, "MIT Engineers Design a Robotic Replica of the Heart's Right Chamber," *Massachusetts Institute of Technology*, December 8, 2023. https://news.mit.edu.

CHAPTER TWO: HOW DOES THE MUSCULAR SYSTEM WORK?

3. Quoted in Dan Dickison, "Professors, Students Laser Focused on Treating Muscle Fatigue," *The College Today* (blog), *College of Charleston*, April 25, 2018. https://today.cofc.edu.

CHAPTER THREE: WHAT CAN GO WRONG WITH THE MUSCULAR SYSTEM?

4. Quoted in Nicole Wetsman, "Here's What Really Happens When You Pull a Muscle," *Popular Science*, May 24, 2023. www.popsci.com.

5. Quoted in "Don't Let Muscle Mass Go to Waste," *Harvard Health Publishing*, April 10, 2023. www.health.harvard.edu.

CHAPTER FOUR: WHAT CAN HUMANS DO TO KEEP THE MUSCULAR SYSTEM HEALTHY?

6. Quoted in "Don't Let Muscle Mass Go to Waste."

7. Quoted in Sonya Collins, "The Truth About Stretching," *WebMD*, June 24, 2024. www.webmd.com.

8. Quoted in "How Microtears Help You to Build Muscle Mass," *University Hospitals*, February 5, 2018. www.uhhospitals.org.

FOR FURTHER RESEARCH

BOOKS

Jonas Edwards, *The Muscular System*. New York: Gareth Stevens, 2021.

Tammy Gagne, *The Human Skeletal System*. San Diego, CA: BrightPoint Press, 2025.

Carla Mooney, *Inside the Human Body*. White River Junction, VT: Nomad, 2020.

INTERNET SOURCES

Rick Ansorge, "Rest and Recovery Are Critical for an Athlete's Physiological and Psychological Well-Being," *UCHealth*, February 7, 2022. www.uchealth.org.

"Healthy Muscles Matter," *National Institute of Arthritis and Musculoskeletal and Skin Diseases*, May 2023. www.niams.nih.gov.

Sarah Klemm, "How Teen Athletes Can Build Muscles with Protein," *Academy of Nutrition and Dietetics*, July 21, 2020. www.eatright.org.

WEBSITES

Get Body Smart
www.getbodysmart.com

Get Body Smart provides information about the systems of the human body, including the muscular system.

Innerbody
www.innerbody.com

Innerbody explains how the systems of the human body work using interactive diagrams. One page provides information about the muscular system.

MedlinePlus
https://medlineplus.gov

MedlinePlus is an official website of the US government. It collects a large amount of health information, including information for teenagers.

INDEX

IMAGE CREDITS

ABOUT THE AUTHOR

Samantha S. Bell lives with her family and four cats in the foothills of the Blue Ridge Mountains. She has written more than 150 nonfiction books for young people of all ages. She loves learning about nutrition and exercise and ways to keep her muscles strong and healthy.